German Combat Uniforms

1939=1945

S. R. GORDON-DOUGLAS

ALMARK PUBLISHING CO. LTD., LONDON

First Published—July 1970
Second Edition (revised and expanded) —November 1970
Reprinted—March 1971
Reprinted—July 1971
Reprinted—November 1971

ISBN 0 85524 016 4 (hard cover edition)
ISBN 0 85524 017 2 (paper covered edition)

Printed in Great Britain by
Vale Press Ltd., Mitcham, Surrey CR4 4HR
for the publishers, Almark Publishing Co. Ltd.,
270 Burlington Road, New Malden,
Surrey KT3 4NL, England.

Introduction

THIS publication has been compiled to give the modeller, the enthusiast and the general reader a concise outline of some of the uniforms and personal equipment used by the ground forces of the Third Reich during World War 2. To cover the subject in infinite detail would necessitate many volumes and the difficulty at first was deciding what to include and also what to exclude. Research has shown that there has been more emphasis placed on parade type uniforms and the like in the past and it was considered that the modeller, and wargamer, would probably prefer details of combat equipment and field uniform. The present volume therefore concentrates on this aspect of the subject though it has perforce been necessary to abbreviate some of the detail to contain it in a book of this size.

The many branches of the Army need not be catalogued here, but obviously the reader will understand that only the more important fighting arms have been included. In brief, the subjects covered are Infantry, Armoured troops, Paratroops, and other arms of the service where a noticeably individual style of uniform was worn. It should be noted that the 'armed' SS—or Waffen-SS—was a separate organisation from the Army. Similarly paratroops were a branch of the Luftwaffe. Since these were major fighting arms, however, their uniforms are included in this present volume as far as their combat dress is concerned. Lists of ranks (and where possible their British and U.S. Army equivalents) together with descriptions of the various rank badges and uniform items have been included. Coloured illustrations together with line drawings and extensive photographic coverage give a reasonably broad outline of the subject and should help the reader to recognise the various branches and ranks therein in his further reading. Those pictures which are reproduced by the courtesy of the Imperial War Museum are credited accordingly (IWM) and the negative number is given where known. Prints may be ordered by the reader on application to the Photo-Library, Imperial War Museum, London, S.E.1.

This second edition is in a new revised format and incorporates several amendments and additions. Special thanks for extra information and suggestions are made to Brian Davis and Gerhard Elser. Some extra illustrations and a brief guide to small arms are included in this edition.

CONTENTS

Victory in the West; a rifle section (squad) of a motorised infantry unit
moves up through a Belgian village street during the invasion of France
and Flanders in May 1940. Note the grenades and gas sheet (Gasplane)
cases. The goggles were worn when riding in the half-track carrier or
truck. This unit still wears its regimental number on the shoulder strap
though this practice was later discarded for security reasons (IWM).

BACK COVER : An MG 34 team in Russia, 1942. They wear standard
accoutrements as drawn on page 45, with the shelter quarter (poncho)
on the rear braces (IWM).

BELOW: Front and rear views of infantrymen in 1936 at the time of the
re-occupation of the de-militarized Rhineland. They are in full marching
order and wear the noticeably larger 1916 pattern helmet (IWM).

Part 1:
Basic Service Dress

THE design of a uniform must take into consideration many points such as: the arm of service in which it is going to be used, the equipment complementary, to it, camouflage, serviceability and, what is more important, the comfort of the wearer and other practicable considerations. This will immediately become obvious in reference to the illustrations in this book. Contrast, for instance, the difference between an infantryman, who has to carry with him a great deal of combat, survival and personal equipment to make himself a single unit, and tankmen with their need to clamber in and out of their fighting vehicles, who could not be encumbered with the equipment appropriate to the infantry. Again, the paratroops and also mountain troops required uniforms which answered to the specialised conditions in which they operated.

ARMY UNIFORM

The general field service uniform was made up of a suitable tunic for combat operations which differed considerably from the parade tunic of the German Army, being lighter in weight and provided with more practical features such as patch pockets. A shirt was worn under the tunic. Trousers, three-quarter length marching boots in leather, and headgear consisting of a service cap, field cap, or steel helmet, completed the basic uniform.

TUNIC PRIOR TO 1943

The tunic (or 'blouse'), originally issued was field grey which actually was a grey-green colour. There was some variation in actual shade of the tunic, depending on its age and amount of cleaning. Also inferior materials used later in the war led to ever faster fading. Thus the shade could be anything from slate grey to a distinct light green and did not always match that of the trousers. The tunic collar could be worn either closed up to the neck or open as the needs required. The collar itself was faced in very dark bottle green material. Under combat conditions the collar was usually worn open and in some cases a scarf of some other neck covering like a camouflaged 'sweat rag' was used. There were large pleated patch pockets in the tunic on either side below the belt, closed by a buttoned flap. This was a development from the first world war when it was found necessary for the troops to leave off much of their equipment during actual fighting and only necessary items of equipment which could be carried in these pockets were taken into action. Two breast pockets of the patch style were also included and they again were of the buttoned over flap type. Front of the tunic was secured by five or six field grey painted buttons.

In contrast with the 1940 scene on page 4 this picture typifies the 1944 style of dress—more casual and less standardised. NCO commander of this light machine gun (MG 34) team, on left, wears the old style tunic with dark green facings, while the other two men wear the 1934 pattern simplified tunic. All wear web gaiters instead of jackboots and the national insignia transfers are missing from the helmets (IWM—JMH126).

STANDARD TUNIC INSIGNIA

The standard insignia were (i) epaulettes, (ii) collar patches and (iii) the national eagle badge. The epaulettes showed the rank together with the arm of service which was indicated by coloured piping. In the case of NCOs and other ranks the base colour of the epaulette was dark green like the collar. The arm of service colour was known throughout the German Army as *Waffenfarbe,* and was repeated on parade tunics in the form of more piping around the collar, around the cap and similarly around the cuff patches. It was also included around the collar patches. A list showing these various colours and their appropriate arms of service is included in Part 3 of this book. Only officers had full piping on their service tunics as described above for parade (or 'uniform') tunics. Other ranks wore *Waffenfarbe* only on their epaulettes in service dress.

A standardised patch was worn on each side of the collar, consisting of a double bar woven in silver-grey thread and with a central strip in each bar in the *Waffenfarbe* colour. This was known as *Doppellitze.* After 1940 these colour strips were discontinued and the bars remained plain

6

silver-grey only, though the older style of collar patch was still to be seen, of course. This did not apply to officers who—by private purchase—continued to wear the old style *Doppellitze* patches. In the Luftwaffe, NCOs had a silver border round two sides of the patch at the points of the greatcoat collar and in the case of specialists the appropriate colour was woven into the border. Officers' collar bars were of a similar style but in silver braid, while all general officers had collar patches in bright red with a stylised gold oak leaf embroidery in lace.

National emblem on the tunic was the styled eagle badge worn over the right breast pocket by all ranks in the Army. (For differences in Waffen-SS and Luftwaffe paratroop tunics and badges see later note.)

TROUSERS

The trousers, as previously mentioned, were of dark grey material initially and thus darker in shade than the tunic. During 1942, however, to reduce costs and material, trousers made of the same field grey material as the tunic were introduced for new issue and from this time on both types of trousers were to be seen, the field grey predominating as time went on. The trousers were tucked into the three-quarter length black leather boots, these are the so-called 'jackboots' universally known especially to people with memories of the 1939-45 period. Once again, however, material shortages forced a change, and from late 1943 the issue of jackboots to other ranks ceased. Leather had become a precious commodity for industrial use. In place of jackboots, black ankle

LEFT: Unteroffizier of signal troops in 1940. Yellow Waffenfarbe and silver braid of an Unteroffizier give the illusion of very wide braiding. Note the 1916 pattern helmet. The specialist badge of a pigeon handler can be seen on the lower right sleeve (see page 44).

BELOW: Unteroffiziers in 1940. They wear the Feldmütze forage cap. The two figures at the left have the pre-1936 type of pointed epaulettes, while the others have rounded ends. (IWM—JMH118).

RIGHT: German infantry in Russia, 1944. Note the gaiters modelled on the British pattern, the simplified 1943 pattern tunic, the mud-daubed helmet, and the web band intended to hold foliage, etc, for camouflage. Weapon is the MP 38 (IWM—M9935). BELOW: A close view of the Feldmütze (forage cap), sleeve badge (two shown), and epaulette of an infantry Oberschutze (private first class). The pre-1936 pointed style epaulette is shown, complete with regimental number. Epaulette was detachable for cleaning, and fixing on top coat, etc (IWM).

boots were issued and these were worn with canvas anklets very similar in pattern to the British type. The jackboot was by no means displaced entirely, however. The black leather belt was worn by all non-commissioned ranks. Officer's belts were brown and additionally, they wore a cross-belt over the right shoulder, though this was discontinued after 1940.

RIGHT: German prisoners in Russia, late 1943, showing clearly the contrast between the 1943 pattern tunic (plain collar and epaulettes, no pleats in pockets) with the earlier tunic worn by the man second from left. Man on extreme left wears a toques (IWM).

FRONT COVER: MG 34 LMG team in Russia, late summer 1943. The gunner, a grenadier, is in the 1943 pattern uniform with anklets instead of jackboots. In the background the team commander, an unteroffizier carries a MP 40 (Picture from the wartime 'Signal' magazine, Brian D a v i s collection).

1943 PATTERN TUNIC

The economies which led to uniform changes as the war progressed had the most profound effect on the tunic which was simplified considerably in 1943 and issued from the latter part of that year. The pleats were removed from the patch pockets, the flaps were reduced in depth, and all the dark bottle green facing material was omitted from the collar and epaulettes. The *Waffenfarbe* remained on the epaulettes, but was retained on the collar only as bars between the silver braid bars. There were six buttons on the front of the new tunic. In 1944, further economies led to some tunics being issued without *Waffenfarbe* or collar patches. However, the earlier pattern tunic continued to be worn and issued (while stocks remained) until the end of the war.

HEADGEAR

The steel helmet 1935 pattern was one of the most characteristic items of equipment associated with the German soldier. Known by many other Armies as a 'coal scuttle' helmet it was the standard issue for all fighting units of the Third Reich with the exception of the airborne troops

ABOVE: MG 34 on tripod mount and with telescopic sight in the medium machine gun role. This 1944 picture shows the inferior quality 1943 pattern tunic being worn by the Obergefreiter in the centre. Note his plain collar and epaulettes. Man on left has the earlier pattern tunic and the metal supports for the belt will be noticed (IWM—JMH115)

who had a specially designed lighter version. The illustrations show the general style of the German helmet. It was a pressed one piece steel type, painted with a grey anti-rust preservative paint. On either side were carried distinctive emblems (shown on pages 17 and 21) which denoted

FAR LEFT: 1935 pattern steel helmet. LEFT: Modified lightweight steel helmet for parachute troops.

the arm of service of the wearer. The Army helmet markings were a shield in national colours (red/white/black) on the right side and a shield with stylised silver eagle-and-swastika on the left. Some units, incidentally, wore 1916 pattern helmets which differed in featuring a lug (intended for a face visor) on each side, and were slightly larger than the 1935 type.

For parade wear and walking out, all ranks wore a peaked service cap (though rarely in wartime) and this was frequently worn by officers on active service as well (and by other ranks on special occasions). On active service the field cap was universally worn by all ranks. This was a fore-and-aft forage cap similar in style to that worn by many other armies. Made of field grey material it was designed so that it could also be worn

Army national badge.

Waffen-SS national badge.

ABOVE LEFT: Two ways of wearing the 1943 pattern Einheitsmütze field cap, showing how sides could be folded. CENTRE: The Feldmutze field cap.

under the steel helmet. Sewn on the front of the cap was the national eagle insignia (as on the tunic) and a rosette *(Reichskokarde)* in red/white/black national colours, beneath an inverted chevron of *Waffenfarbe* arm of service piping. Officers also had silver piping along the seams of the crown and edges of the turn-up but for generals this was replaced by gold piping. In 1943 a new field cap was introduced (the *Einheitsmütze*) which was based closely on the style of peaked cap worn by mountain troops and Afrika Korps (see Part 2). The eagle insignia was carried on the crown above the rosette in national colours. The *Einheitsmütze* subsequently became the most widely worn type of headgear on active service and appeared in camouflaged forms also in certain arms. The sides folded down and buttoned under the chin in cold weather.

BELOW, LEFT: This 1941 picture shows to advantage the 1935 pattern helmet and the silver braided epaulettes and collar patches of an infantry Leutnant (IWM—JMH141). RIGHT: Rubber tyre inner tubes cut up to form bands were often used on the helmet to hold camouflage garnishing. These are assault engineers during the invasion of France, May 1940.

ABOVE LEFT: Buckle for service belt, worn by Army and Luftwaffe officers. RIGHT: Buckle for service belt, worn by NCOs and other ranks.

LEFT. MG 34 crew in Russia 1942. Man on far left carries the tripod. Note helmets slung from belt (IWM). LEFT, BOTTOM: Artillery gun crew wearing abbreviated equipment of belt, bayonet frog, and respirator container, France, April 1944. Oberkanonier (far right) wears the 1943 pattern tunic but the NCO far left has the earlier tunic. RIGHT: Waffen-SS Panzer-Grenadiers in 1942, wearing the Army style tunic. Note the folded camouflage smocks attached to their belts, the regimental armband, and the distinctive helmet marking and eagle emblem. On right is an Unterscharführer. Weapons shown are the '08 Luger pistol and Kar 98K rifle. (IWM—STT-1599).

WAFFEN-SS STANDARD UNIFORM

The Waffen-SS was virtually a 'private' army organised separately from the German Army (Heer) though its equipment, organisation, and training, were similar. It had its own badges of rank and emblems (see Part 3) and variations in uniform, however. In the years just prior to the war all ranks wore a field tunic in brown-grey which was based in cut on the current black service uniform of the SS. This had a turned-back collar with rank and arm insignia indicated on patches on the revers. With this tunic a brown or grey shirt and black tie was worn. In the 1937-39 period this began to be replaced by a new tunic in field grey which buttoned up to the neck and had a turn-down collar still featuring the rank patches. On active service the collar could be worn open with the top button undone. This tunic retained the slanting side pockets of the earlier tunics. By 1940-41, however, an Army-style tunic was on general issue with turn-down collar (and under-shirt) as previously described.

The major distinction was the national eagle emblem which was in a different style (see page 11) and was worn on the left arm instead of on the right breast as in the Army. The Waffen-SS field cap was of a slightly different style from the Army cap, being more streamlined in cut and with shallower turn-ups. The national eagle emblem was frequently worn on the left side of their cap, though this was not universal and it could be

RIGHT: Army pattern tunic worn by Waffen-SS artillery men. Note distinctive belt plate and helmet emblem, also the rank and SS insignia on the collar. FOOT OF PAGE: Buckles for service belts of Waffen-SS officer (left) and other ranks (right).

seen on the front of the crown as on the Army cap. The later peaked field cap was also adopted by the Waffen-SS and the badge was, once again, often worn on the left side. In place of the rosette on all Waffen-SS caps a metal or embroidered 'death's head' badge was worn. Officers' caps were piped in silver-grey as in the Army though field and junior officers wore white piping until the end of 1940. For other specialised clothing peculiar to the Waffen-SS see Part 2.

RIGHT: Luftwaffe Flak-artillerie crew in a night action, wearing top coats. Note the red collar patches. They are carrying obsolete pattern haversack-type anti-gas respirators instead of the cylindrical metal carriers issued to first-line units. BELOW: The Luftwaffe Fliegermutze forage cap was of more streamlined cut than the Army forage cap.

LUFTWAFFE

Luftwaffe uniforms in general are beyond the scope of this book and on active service paratroops wore the 'jump' dress described in Part 2. When not so attired, however, they wore Luftwaffe service dress which was blue-grey in colour similar in cut to Army dress, though the tunic had a turnback collar. The forage cap was of the shallow type, similar to that worn by the Waffen-SS. The national eagle emblem, worn on the cap and right breast, was in 'flying' pose and was also marked on the helmet side (as illustrated). The leather belt and equipment was brown before the war, but black equipment replaced it in the early war years. The Luftwaffe Flak units also wore the standard Luftwaffe service dress and equipment, as did Luftwaffe units serving as infantry. The alternative garment to service dress, and very commonly worn was the *Fliegerbluse*, a one-piece fly-front combination suit originally introduced for aircrew. The *Fliegerbluse* was standard wear (beneath the smock) for paratroops, and was frequent wear for Flak troops. It was blue-grey in colour, and rank badge collar patches, plus the Luftwaffe breast eagle, were worn on this garment in the 'standard' positions.

Ranks were indicated on epaulettes and collar patches, and piping (and the patches themselves) were coloured to indicate the branch. For Flak troops the colour was red.

LEFT, BELOW: Range taker of Luftwaffe Flakartillerie in Fleigermütze cap and grey overalls. BELOW: Obergefreiter of Luftwaffe Flakartillerie in Einheitsmutze and service dress (IWM—JMH387).

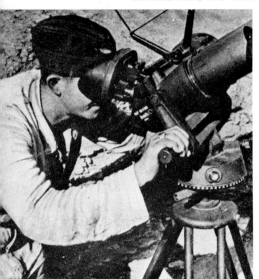 

TOP COATS

The overcoat *(mantel)* was of a standard pattern throughout the German Army, worn by officers, NCOs and other ranks alike with only detail differences to account for rank insignia, etc. In style it was a very long double breasted garment, buttoned up to the neck, and was field grey in colour. The collar for the Army was a dark bottle green, and plain for the Waffen-SS. It had grey metal buttons except for general officers who had gilded ones. The epaulettes were as in use on the field service tunic, piped in the appropriate *Waffenfarbe.* General officers also wore the two top buttons undone showing, in the Army, bright red facings, and in the Waffen-SS a very pale grey. There was a short buttoned-over half belt at the back above a double pleated vent. The service or parade leather belt was usually worn on the outside when the overcoat was used. Towards the end of the war a new pattern overcoat was issued, of simpler cut and distinguished by its very wide collar.

The leather coat was similar in style to the overcoat but shorter, and was grey in colour. Usually no rank markings were carried on the leather coat but occasionally epaulettes were fitted by the wearer.

RIGHT: An MG 34 team in top coats. Man on left carries a drum-type magazine (MG-Trommel) slung from his belt. Man on far right with MP 40 wears the long magazine carriers for this weapon on his belt instead of the normal small pouches. FAR RIGHT: Pre-war parade with top coats being worn. Note cross-belt for officers, discontinued in 1940.

16

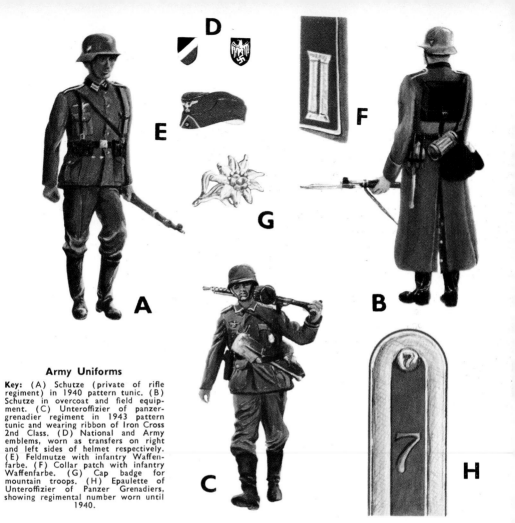

Army Uniforms

Key: (A) Schutze (private of rifle regiment) in 1940 pattern tunic. (B) Schutze in overcoat and field equipment. (C) Unteroffizier of panzergrenadier regiment in 1943 pattern tunic and wearing ribbon of Iron Cross 2nd Class. (D) National and Army emblems, worn as transfers on right and left sides of helmet respectively. (E) Feldmutze with infantry Waffenfarbe. (F) Collar patch with infantry Waffenfarbe. (G) Cap badge for mountain troops. (H) Epaulette of Unteroffizier of Panzer Grenadiers, showing regimental number worn until 1940.

Part 2: Special Service Uniforms

BESIDES the standard service uniforms described in Part 1, there were uniforms distinctive to certain special arms (eg, panzer and mountain troops) or for special purposes (eg, fatigues or camouflage) and climates.

ARMOURED TROOPS

Mechanised and armoured troops wore a shorter double-breasted style field jacket and for those serving with armoured cars and tanks the distinctive black colour is well known. The trousers, also black, were fastened around the ankle and were usually tucked into ankle boots, though they were sometimes just gathered in and worn with laced shoes. The headgear varied considerably especially as the War progressed and as other uniform designs became included in the equipment of these troops. Originally a black beret with foam rubber padding was the style used but this soon went out of use (in late 1940) and was replaced

XXII 3. 6.

LEFT: Tank crews in black panzer suits being inspected by General Von Bock. Note leather coat, left (IWM). BELOW: Captured Sturmgeschütze crew man (right) in field grey combination suit. (IWM). BELOW LEFT: Tank crew man in black panzer suit and SP gun crew man in field grey suit.

LEFT: Waffen-SS panzer troops in 1940, wearing old style panzer beret with protective crash liner which was discarded that year. Note the SS runes on the right collar patch and the eagle emblem on the left arm, with 'death's head' badge under the eagle emblem on the cap (IWM—JMH125).

by the field cap as already described but in the 'Panzer Black'. Here again the *Einheitsmütze* with a peak was used from about mid-1943 and this same style of cap was also issued in camouflage material, to Waffen-SS tank units. The rank badges of the armoured troops were the same as those for the rest of the Army with the exception of the collar patches which were black with a dull aluminium 'death's head' device in the centre. Waffen-SS panzer units wore on the right collar patch the SS runes in silver embroidery and their own distinctive rank markings on the left

Above: (A) Infantryman in spring pattern camouflage shelter quarter and helmet cover, with Panzerfaust. (B) Panzer troops NCO with MP38 and wearing ribbon of Iron Cross 2nd Class. (C) General Oberst in overcoat. (D) Panzer troops padded cap, worn until 1940. (E) Major of artillery, epaulette. (F) Officer's service cap, infantry, with white Waffenfarbe.

Waffen-SS Uniforms

Opposite page: (A) Sturmbannführer of artillery troops 3rd SS-Panzer (Totenkopf) Division, with enlarged view of left arm badges. Chevron and star on right arm indicate previous service with army or police. (B) National insignia worn as a transfer on left side of steel helmet by Waffen-SS. (C) Sturmmann of SS-Panzer troops; note eagle emblem on left side of forage cap. (D) Untersturmführer in SS pattern camouflage smock. (E)
(Continued opposite)

patch again in silver. The epaulettes, collar patches, collar, and cap piping for armoured troops were all of the pink *Panzer Waffenfarben*. This included Waffen-SS.

Assault gun (Sturmgeschütz) troops wore the same style of uniform but made of field grey material throughout. This same style of uniform was brought out later in camouflage material by the Waffen-SS and was worn from late 1943 by Waffen-SS tank and assault gun crews. A camouflage cap in the *Einheitsmütze* pattern was issued with the camouflage suit and this was reversible with autumn and spring/summer patterns as described on page 22.

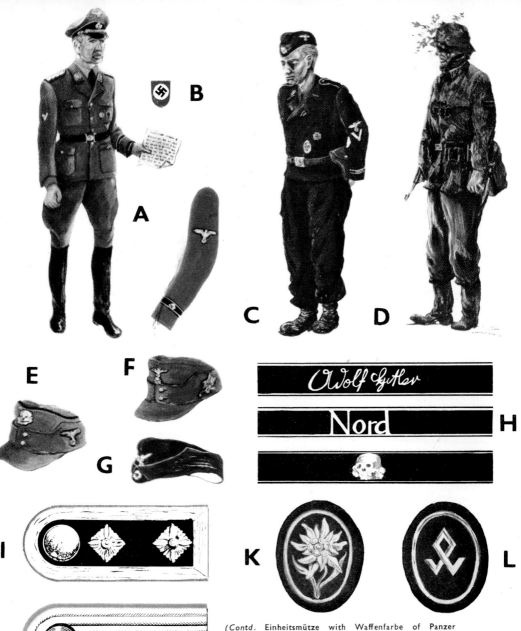

(Contd. from page 20) Einheitsmütze with Waffenfarbe of Panzer engineer troops. (F) Gebirgsmutze of Waffen-SS mountain troops, showing light green Waffenfarbe. (G) Feldmutze of SS-Panzer troops; eagle emblem could be worn on left side as in drawing C. (H) Typical divisional arm bands for 1st SS-Panzer (Adolf Hitler), 6th SS-Mountain (Nord) and 3rd SS-Panzer (Totenkopf) Divisions, worn on left cuff as in drawing C. (I) Hauptscharführer of SS-Panzer troops, epaulette. (J) Untersturmführer of Waffen-SS mountain infantry troops, epaulette. (K) Arm badge of SS mountain troops (right arm). (L) Arm badge of 'Prinz Eugen' division, worn by Oberführer and above on left arm, in place of collar patch worn by lower ranks.

Victorious paratroops in Holland, May 1940, wearing the plain grey-green smocks with zip pockets—see also the colour drawing on page 25 and the drawings on page 45. Note the mud daubed on helmets for camouflage. The man in the centre is carrying a belt of ammunition for the MG 34. Note that the man on the extreme left is an ex-Army parachutist and wears the Army eagle emblem on his breast rather than the Luftwaffe emblem.

SMOCKS

Smocks were worn by both the Luftwaffe paratroops and the Waffen-SS infantry and panzer-grenadier units. Originally the paratroops wore a blue-grey *Fliegerbluse* over which was worn a rush green (grey-green) smock. This was used in the 1939-41 period. The smock was just over knee length but could be fastened up around the top of the wearer's legs so that the parachute harness would not be fouled when jumping. It had zip breast pockets. Later a camouflaged smock of similar pattern (but lacking the zip pockets) was issued with a green/brown 'splinter' type pattern. By 1943 most Luftwaffe parachute units were deployed in the ground fighting role (the opportunities for airborne operations having diminished) and a combat dress more suitable for the new role was adopted. This featured a shortened smock in camouflage pattern with the blue-grey *Fliegerbluse* or drill trousers gathered into ankle boots. A camouflage helmet cover was also issued, but the paratroop lightweight helmet was retained.

The Waffen-SS smock differed entirely in pattern from the original Luftwaffe smock. It had elasticated cuffs, was tunic length and collarless,

ABOVE: Luftwaffe Paratroops in 1942 camouflage smock and jump suit (left) and in 1944 camouflage smock and drill trousers for ground fighting role. LEFT: Parachutist in the long 'splinter' camouflage smock and with sweat rag at neck. BELOW: Oberst (colonel) Brauer confers with an unteroffizier in Crete.

ABOVE: Paratroops running for cover immediately on landing during the invasion of Holland, May 1940. RIGHT: A pre-war picture of Army parachutists in training, showing the zip pockets in the smock and the arrangement of the parachute harness.

LEFT: Luftwaffe parachutists of the 1943 period in the smock, worn here with drill tropical trousers (IWM— MH6345).

Luftwaffe Uniforms

Right: Oberfeldwebel (Oberwachtmeister) of Luftwaffe Flakartillerie wearing service dress and the long pouches for Schmeisser magazines used with the MP 38 or MP 40. **Far right:** Gefreiter of Luftwaffe parachute troops in early (1940) pattern smock. He carries the FG 42 (Fallschirmjaegerewehr 42) gun. **Below:** Two Luftwaffe cuff titler; Hermann Göring Panzer Division and Fallschirmjager (parachute) Regiment No. 1.

HERMANN GÖRING | Fallschirm-Jäger-Rgt. 1

and had a lace up neck. It was worn over the standard tunic and had slits to give access to the tunic pockets. The tunic collar was worn outside the smock. This Waffen-SS smock was also reversible; it had a 'mottled' pattern of brown/grey/tan on one side for autumn wear, and a similar pattern featuring mainly green/brown and brick pink on the other side for spring and summer wear. The Waffen-SS camouflage pattern, first introduced in 1939-40, was thus quite distinct from the 'splinter' pattern later used by the Army and Luftwaffe. A similar reversible helmet cover in matching patterns was issued with the smock. It is of interest to note that Waffen-SS parachute units wore a smock of Luftwaffe parachute pattern but with the Waffen-SS camouflage pattern. They wore a field grey coverall or standard service tunic beneath the smock but had a lightweight parachute helmet as for Luftwaffe paratroops. The badges, etc, followed normal Waffen-SS rules for positioning.

OTHER CAMOUFLAGE GARMENTS

The winter smock and trousers was intended for the conditions which that season could bring. Made of two layers of windproof and waterproof cloth with a woollen lining, it had a fitted hood under which could be worn the toques as shown, or the *Einheitsmütze* field service cap in one of the two positions shown on page 11; either right down, or with the

ABOVE: Waffen-SS cavalry of the famous 'Florian Geyer' SS-Kavallerie Division, 1942, in smocks with field grey riding breeches. (IWM-GER55Y).

LEFT: A close view of the Waffen-SS pattern 'mottle' camouflage smock. Rank badge indicates a Sturmann. Also shown is the camouflage cap (IWM—JMH342).
ABOVE: Waffen-SS motorised infantry in standard camouflage 'mottle' smock and helmet cover (IWM—JMH204).

sides turned up, as well. The winter suit was generally worn over the field service uniform. The ammunition pouches, holster, etc. were worn on the normal belt under it. It had patch pockets in the smock part and side pockets in the trousers. Again, like the camouflage smocks it was reversible, all white on one side and camouflaged on the other. The camouflage pattern matched that used on the paratroopers' smocks, being the more angular, 'splinter' type pattern, as previously described. The winter suit was first issued on the Russian front in winter 1942-43 as a result of the bitter experiences of the previous winter. Also to be seen were quilted winter Parkas in field grey which were issued to some special duty men. Some winter suits were also supplied in plain grey.

Coveralls were widely worn by all services and all branches of those services. The coloured illustration shows the camouflaged type issued to Waffen-SS tank men (and other Waffen-SS motorised troops sometimes). This was extensively used from 1943 onwards. The camouflage field service cap was usually worn with it. Basically the coverall was a boiler

BELOW, RIGHT: Rarely shown in pictures is the reverse side of the reversible winter suit. Finished in white on one side, the other side was in 'splinter' camouflage. LEFT: Waffen-SS 81 mm mortar team in Italy, June 1944, wearing camouflage face masks (peculiar to the Waffen-SS) thrown back over their helmets.

AFRIKAKORPS

Above: (A) Oberleutnant, Afrika Korps, wearing standard issue tropical dress. (B) Gefreiter of Afrika Korps in non-standard combination of tropical dress with field tunic. (C) Schutze of Afrika Korps in tropical shorts with field tunic. (D) Hauptmann of mountain troops in reversible smock, white side out. (E) Tropical Einheitsmütze with Panzer Waffen-farbe. (F) Afrika Korps cuff title.

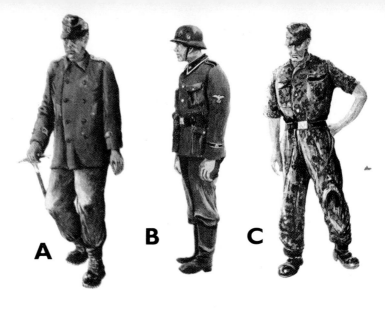

Above: (A) Officer of mountain troops in wind jacket. (B) Unterscharfuhrer of Waffen-SS artillery (red Waffenfarbe) in army pattern tunic. (C) Sturmman of Waffen-SS panzer troops in camouflaged coverall suit and cap. **Below:** (D) Kanonier of Luftwaffe Flakartillerie in brown coverall suit, Russian Front 1943, with helmet overpainted brown. (E) Oberleutnant of assault gun (sturmgeschutze) troops wearing assault and wound badges on left breast (beneath Iron Cross) and with ribbon of East Medal in lapel.

TOP OF PAGE: Issued for special duties was the quilted green Parka suit, as worn here by an artillery observation officer in Russia (IWM—STT-2381). ABOVE: Two toques (a wrap-around scarf) for wear under the helmet or hood in winter conditions. FAR LEFT: The reversible winter suit, the toques, the white-washed helmet were features of the second winter in Russia, 1942-43 (IWM—JMH222). LEFT: Another view of the winter suit, this time worn with the hood up. This hood was detachable.

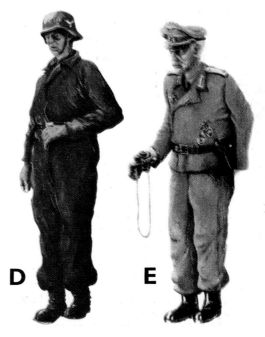

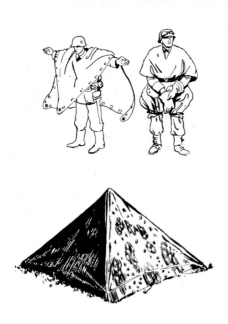

TOP LEFT: The camouflage shelter quarter shown in use as a 'poncho' or rain cape. On universal issue it was used by all fighting arms of the Army. Drawings show four erected as a shelter and method of wearing (IWM—GER9Y). ABOVE RIGHT: Sheepskin coats were issued for special duties (eg, sentries) on the Western Front during the first winter of the war, 1939-40. These luxuries were in short supply. Note the 1916 pattern helmets.

suit with two fairly large breast patch pockets, and two side pockets in the trouser part. As with the other camouflaged uniforms the pattern was the same. The same style of coverall was used by Luftwaffe Flak (anti-aircraft) troops but the colour varied. Originally it was in the Luftwaffe blue/grey, but some coveralls in a dark reddish brown were issued. Waffen-SS tank men were issued with a camouflaged blouse of the same style and pattern as the double breasted Panzer type (page 20). On this garment the special rank insignia for camouflaged dress appeared. Officially rank badges were not allowed on the camouflaged coveralls, but they frequently appeared none the less.

In 1944 a complete camouflage suit was introduced for the Waffen-SS and became widely worn by Waffen-SS infantry units in the last year of the war. The suit consisted of a tunic and trousers similar in cut and style to the Army-pattern standard uniform but it was made throughout in cheap drill material. With it was worn the peaked camouflage cap in matching pattern. Two different camouflage patterns were produced, one more 'green' than the other and the pattern had a distinct 'mottle' finish. Jackboots were not worn with this; ankle boots and puttees were worn instead, typical of the economy then prevailing in Germany. Rank badges were not officially permitted to be worn with this suit, but in practice they usually were.

One other camouflage garment, widely used, was the winter snow

A good comparison between the Waffen-SS 'mottled' camouflage pattern and the Army 'splinter' camouflage. LEFT: Waffen-SS infantry are shown carrying equipment suspended from waist belt and with trousers worn outside jackboots. RIGHT: The shelter quarter in normal wear as a 'poncho' by a member of a field artillery crew (IWM).

coverall which was a two piece white suit consisting of an overall smock with hood and overall trousers. This suit was worn over existing uniform clothing as required. It was a thin linen garment (not to be confused with the winter suit previously described) which merely provided a snow camouflage rather than protection against the cold. In the first winter of the war, at least, an extemporised snow camouflage cover was sometimes worn in the form of a white cape. Occasionally a white cloth helmet cover was used, or helmets were whitewashed, but such extemporised snow camouflage measures were used throughout the war to some extent.

CAMOUFLAGE SHELTER

The Camouflage Shelter Quarter (or 'poncho') was a piece of equipment very extensively used. Simple in design, but very useful in operation, it was triangular in shape, measuring 8' 3" x 8' 3" x 6' 3". The coloured illustration (page 20) shows it being worn as a 'poncho' by the wearer putting his head through a hole in the middle. The small line drawings show the method of putting it on. It could be worn by a motorised trooper belted around the knees and the waist, and also, as shown, four could be made into a very serviceable tent. It was intended, as well, for use as a groundsheet. The camouflage pattern, as for the smocks, was reversible, for autumn or summer/spring. The appropriate side was worn outwards as necessary. Any number of shelter quarters could be buttoned together to form a long communal bivouac for a complete squad of men.

MOUNTAIN TROOPS

Mountain troops wore a basic tunic and trousers following the standard Army pattern. They had a distinctive peaked mountain service cap (the *Bergmütze*). This had turned-down side flaps which could be buttoned

under the chin. A similar pattern cap which was adopted for general issue to the Army (and Waffen-SS) in 1943 as the *Einheitsmütze* as previously described, though the style was very slightly modified. The *Eidelweis* flower was adopted as the mountain troops' emblem and this was worn as either a metal or embroidered silver badge on the left side of the *Bergemütze*. The *Eidelweis* was also featured in the mountain troops' badge worn on the right arm.

Special clothing was also issued to mountain troops to meet the extreme climatic conditions in which they operated. Standard issue was a sage green waterproof wind jacket which was double breasted, loose

ABOVE: Mountain troops light machine gun team (with MG 42) showing the Bergmütze cap and Eidelweis badge. Top coats are being worn (IWM—JMH126). RIGHT: Mountain division artillery battery on the march. Note method of slinging rifles.

fitting, and reached to the thighs. A reversible camouflage smock was also issued which had white lining and a hood. It was worn with the white outside when operating above the snow line. Ski or climbing boots were issued instead of jackboots and these were worn with puttees. In the early part of the war pictorial evidence shows that knee length 'Alpine trousers' and long woollen stockings were sometimes worn.

LEFT: Commander (Generalmajor) of 3rd Mountain Division (centre) with his staff officers, 1940. Note his collar patches, and the various ways of wearing the puttees (IWM—GER1265). RIGHT: Jäger and Oberschütze (right) of a mountain regiment demonstrate method of skiing with injured man. Note absence of Eidelweis badge in this case (IWM—JMH326).

AFRIKA KORPS AND SUMMER DRESS

The Afrika Korps used a great variety of different types of clothing in the North Africa campaign, 1941-43. Most of it was originally peculiar to the desert and not often found in other theatres of the war. It was also common practice in this area for the forces of all the participants to use captured unorthodox, and in many cases, non-military articles of clothing which were based more on personal choice and comfort rather than fixed rules and regulations. This makes pictorial evidence rather untrustworthy but there were standards of issue which must be mentioned.

Headgear varied with the period. The tropical pith helmet, in olive green felt with the same arm-of-service and national transfers as on the steel helmet, was worn generally at the early stages in 1941. See the illustrations for examples. Rules for emblem application were as described

RIGHT: The standard tropical service uniform, here being worn by sentries in Crete. On the right is a senior Obergefreiter (over six years service) and on the left is a Leutnant. Note the piping on the officer's Einheitsmütze (c a p) (IWM—JMH236).

for the steel helmet. The pith helmet, however, soon proved cumbersome and of dubious value. Like the British, the Afrika Korps discarded this item of uniform after a few months experience and reverted to caps of the same pattern as worn in Europe.

The field service cap, patterned on that worn by the mountain battalions, was in general use because it was admirably suited to the conditions of the desert. Also in use was the field cap (tropical) which had no visor and was the same style as the standard field cap except that it was in light twill material.

Colours tended to vary quite considerably as the bleaching effect of the sun and desert was severe. Usually uniforms and caps were issued in either a light olive green or sand colour, but after some period of service they faded to lighter shades of brown and green. In many cases they ended up as a natural fabric tone.

The uniforms suffered the same fate as the headgear and what was common practice towards the latter half of the campaign was not particularly true for the early stages. Originally the Afrika Korps were issued with a regulation tropical uniform comprised of a green/olive field tunic with khaki shirt, drill shorts, knee length stockings, and canvas topped lace-up boots. There were also alternative long trousers, in khaki drill which were worn full length, gathered in at the ankle into normal leather boots. Officers usually wore the standard pattern riding breeches, but in khaki twill, tucked into the top of the tropical boots.

Cut of the tropical tunic was similar to that of the European one,

LEFT: The tropical service uniform as worn by the Afrika K o r p s. Gefreiter on right and Obergefreiter in centre. Note the lace-up boots and the goggles. Man on left wears non-regulation jersey and shorts (IWM—BM3748).

complete with patch pockets. However, it was open at the neck with the standard collar patches in thread sewn on to the revers. The tunic could be worn with shirt and tie but frequently either the shirt or tunic was left off and sweat rags were commonly worn at the neck. Belts and accoutrements issued with tropical uniforms were of webbing material.

All rank markings and other insignia were worn on the tunic in the appropriate place and a green and silver 'Afrika Korps' cuff title was carried on the right sleeve if appropriate. The national insignia eagle emblem was the same pattern as for all other theatres but instead of being silver (white) on a dark green backing, it was grey on a light tan cloth, silver for colonels, and gold for generals.

In 1942, by which time German conquests covered much of southern Europe, southern Russia, and the Balkans, the tropical dress introduced for North Africa became the standard summer dress for all warm climes. Except for the discarded pith helmet the issue was identical in all respects to the issue for North Africa. Waffen-SS followed their normal style for the position of badges so that the eagle emblem was worn on the left sleeve and often on the left of the *Einheitsmütze*. Even in northern Europe this summer dress was worn by some units when appropriate, for example at Normandy in mid-1944 when some German troops were wearing summer dress. In the latter part of the war items of summer dress issue were to be seen worn in various combinations, frequently with parts of the European service uniform. For example the drill trousers might be worn with the field grey tunic or a camouflage smock. Waffen-SS units did not serve with Afrika Korps but wore tropical uniforms in other theatres.

The most common German Army uniform styles contrasted; the crew of the StuG IV are wearing the field grey combination 'panzer suit' with respectively a Feldmütze, Einheitsmütze, and service cap headgear. In the foreground are an NCO with helmet, an officer wearing breeches and an Einheitsmütze, and an officer with service cap.

Part 3:
Badges and Insignia

THIS section of the book illustrates a selection of main rank insignia and some principal decorations. However, this is really a subject in itself beyond the scope of the present volume, so the coverage here is restricted only to the most important items.

Standard tunic and helmet insignia have necessarily been referred to in the description of the uniform. These consisted of the national eagle emblem *(Hoheitsabzeichen)* on the tunic front and headwear, or on the left sleeve in the case of the Waffen-SS, and the national colours of red/white/black in a rosette on the cap and a shield on the helmet (Army and Luftwaffe only). In the Army and Waffen-SS the arm of service was indicated by the distinctive *Waffenfarbe* piping, a list of which is given here. Its positioning has already been described.

Rank and specialisation were thus denoted on the epaulettes (Army and Luftwaffe), but the junior non-commissioned ranks also had sleeve badges as illustrated. In the Waffen-SS, apart from the epaulettes and sleeve badges, further indication of rank was given by the left-hand collar patch, examples, again being given. In September 1942, new style

Table 1 : Uniform Terms Summarised

English	German	Remarks
Pack	Tornister	Canvas with leather binding
Tunic/blouse	Feldbluse	
Trousers	Hosen	
Overcoat	Mantel	
Steel helmet	Stahlhelm	1935 or 1916 pattern
Field cap	Feldmütze	Original fore-and-aft type
Mountain cap	Bergemütze	Peaked
Field cap (peaked)	Einheitsmütze	Derived from mountain cap, adopted 1943
Field cap (Luftwaffe)	Fleigermütze	Differed from Army pattern
National eagle	Hoheitsabzeichen (Army) Hoheitszeichen (Luftwaffe)	
Rosette (caps)	Reichskokarde	Not in Waffen-SS
Arm of service colour	Waffenfarbe	See Table 2
Flying suit	Fliegerbluse	Luftwaffe only

rank patches in much simplified form were introduced for wear on the later types of uniform such as smocks. These badges were in various combinations of bars and oak leaves and were worn on the left sleeve. Examples are given. The Luftwaffe already had a similar type of badge system with stylised wings instead of bars, originally worn on the collar patches of the service tunic. On paratroop smocks similar badges were worn on both sleeves.

All generals wore red patches with gold embroidered oak leaf design and the bright red *Waffenfarbe.* On the side seams of the trousers Army generals wore a double red stripe (giving the appearance of a single broad stripe from afar). Similarly, Luftwaffe generals wore white stripes, and staff officers of both the Army and Luftwaffe wore carmine red stripes.

Regimental numbers, originally worn on the epaulettes were discarded for security reasons when the war started. However, divisional identity was later established (partly for morale reasons) by the issue of cuff titles to some Army divisions. This was common practice in Waffen-SS divisions, whose cuff titles had been in use since before the war.

LEFT: Generalmajor (foreground) with the distinctive general's red/gold collar patch, with an Oberst (behind him) and a Hauptmann, plus other officers, watching exercises in France, April 1944. Note that they wear white neck sweat bands (Bellona-Warpics).

RIGHT: Badges of rank worn on both upper arms in special camouflage clothing by Waffen-SS. Colour was light green on a black background. Same badges were used by Army personnel in camouflage clothing.

Sturmscharfuhrer

Hauptscharfuhrer

Oberscharfuhrer

Hauptsturmfuhrer

Obersturmfuhrer

Untersturmfuhrer

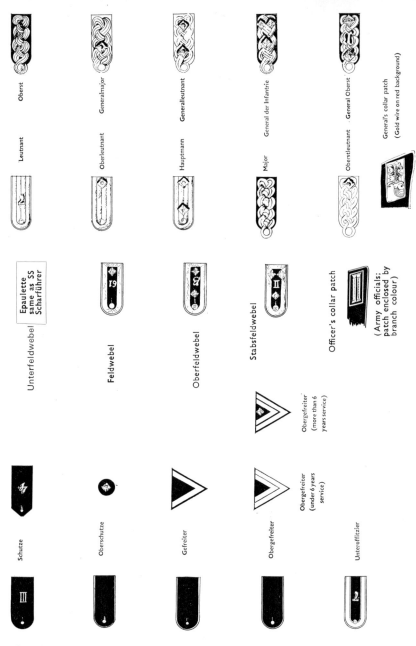

Oberst

Generalmajor

Generalleutnant

General der Infantrie

General Oberst

General's collar patch
(Gold wire on red background)

Leutnant

Oberleutnant

Hauptmann

Major

Oberstleutnant

Unterfeldwebel | Epaulette same as SS Scharführer

Feldwebel

Oberfeldwebel

Stabsfeldwebel

Officer's collar patch

(Army officials; patch enclosed by branch colour)

Obergefreiter (more than 6 years service)

Schutze

Oberschutze

Gefreiter

Obergefreiter

Obergefreiter (under 6 years service)

Unteroffizier

ABOVE: Badges of rank for Army personnel. The pre-1936 pattern pointed epaulette is shown for a Schutze. The regimental numbers were dropped from epaulettes soon after the start of the war but examples are shown. The 'star' for an Oberschutze and chevrons for the Gefreiter and Obergefreiter were worn on the left upper arm.

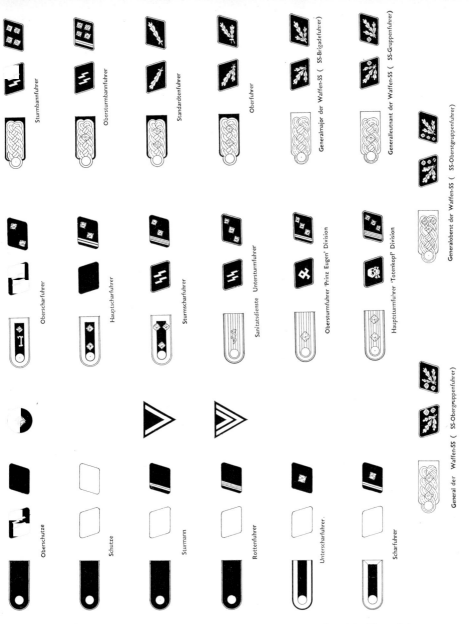

ABOVE: Rank badges and distinctions of the Waffen-SS. The plain out-line or black collar patch drawn for some ranks indicates a repetition of the collar patch immediately above. Note that certain divisions wore a distinctive collar patch emblem in place of the runic SS symbol, and two examples are shown. From Standartenführer upwards, rank badges were worn on both collar patches The 'star' of the Oberschütze and chevrons of the Sturmmann and Rottenführer were worn on the left upper arm.

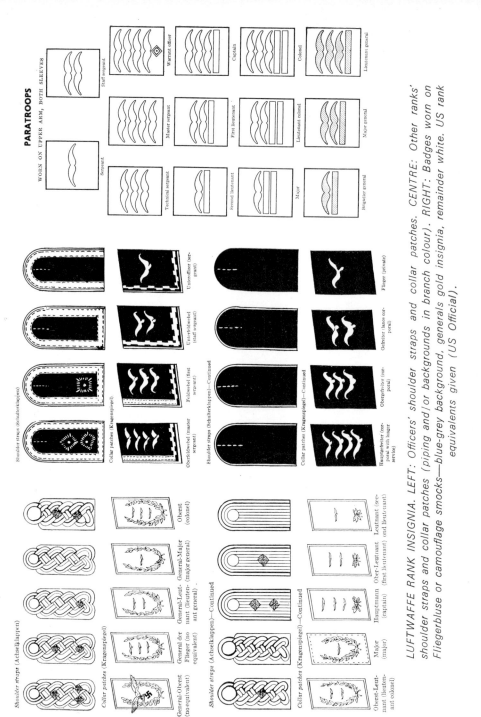

PARATROOPS

WORN ON UPPER ARM, BOTH SLEEVES

Sergeant

Staff sergeant

Technical sergeant

Master sergeant

Warrant officer

Second lieutenant

First lieutenant

Captain

Major

Lieutenant colonel

Colonel

Brigadier general

Major general

Lieutenant general

Shoulder straps (Schulterklappen)

Collar patches (Kragenspiegel)

Unteroffizier (sergeant)

Unterfeldwebel (staff sergeant)

Feldwebel (first sergeant)

Oberfeldwebel (master sergeant)

Shoulder straps (Schulterklappen)—Continued

Collar patches (Kragenspiegel)—Continued

Flieger (private)

Gefreiter (lance corporal)

Obergefreiter (corporal)

Hauptgefreiter (corporal with longer service)

Shoulder straps (Achselklappen)

Collar patches (Kragenspiegel)

General der Flieger (no equivalent)

General-Leutnant (lieutenant general)

General-Major (major general)

Oberst (colonel)

General-Oberst (no equivalent)

Shoulder straps (Achselklappen)—Continued

Collar patches (Kragenspiegel)—Continued

Oberst-Leutnant (lieutenant colonel)

Major (major)

Hauptmann (captain)

Ober-Leutnant (first lieutenant)

Leutnant (second lieutenant) and lieutenant

LUFTWAFFE RANK INSIGNIA. LEFT: Officers' shoulder straps and collar patches. CENTRE: Other ranks' shoulder straps and collar patches (piping and/or backgrounds in branch colour). RIGHT: Badges worn on Fliegerbluse or camouflage smocks—blue-grey background, generals gold insignia, remainder white. US rank equivalents given (US Official).

40

Table 2 : Arm of Service Colours (Waffenfarben)

Waffenfarben is a shortening of the word *Waffengatungsfarbe* which roughly translated means 'arm of service colour'. This had been a practice in the German Army for many years and every uniform carried it in some form or other. The adjacent list shows in general the appropriate arm of service alongside the colour:

Arm of Service	Colour
Infantry	White
Armoured Troops, Anti-Tank Units, Armoured Reconnaissance Units	Pink
Cavalry	Golden Yellow
Artillery	Bright Red
General Staff Officers	Carmine Red
Signals	Lemon Yellow
Administrative Officials	Dark Green
Engineers	Black
Panzer Grenadiers	Apple Green
Mountain and Jäger Regiments	Light Green
Medical Corps	Cornflower Blue
Mechanised Supply Troops (also Military Law Officials)	Orange
Recruiting Officers	
Smoke Troops (Rocket Projectors)	Wine Red
Specialist Officers	Grey-Blue
Veterinary Corps	Crimson
Chaplains	Violet

NB: Deviations from regulations included white, pink, or golden yellow for some Panzer Grenadier units, and pink, golden yellow, or copper brown, for armoured reconnaissance units.

The Waffen-SS *Waffenfarben* showed slight variations on the above list, as follows:

Arm of Service	Colour
Cavalry and Motorised Reconnaissance Units	Golden Yellow
Tank and Anti-Tank Troops	Rose Pink
Artillery	Bright Red
Infantry	White
General Officers	Light Grey
Concentration Camp Guards	Light Brown
Veterinary Corps	Crimson
Rifle Regiments of SS Police Divisions	Grass Green
Mountain Infantry	Light Green
Administration	Sky Blue
Engineers	Black
Reserve Officers	Dark Green

Table 3 : Heer (Army) and Waffen-SS ranks and their equivalents

Army (Heer)	Waffen-SS	British	U.S.
Schütze (1)	Schütze	Private	Private
Oberschütze (2)	Oberschütze	Private (senior)	PFC
Gefreiter	Sturmmann	Lance Corporal	Acting Corporal
Obergefreiter	Rottenführer	Corporal	Corporal
Unteroffizier	Uterscharführer	Lance Sergeant	Sergeant
Unterfeldwebel	Scharführer	Sergeant	Staff Sergeant
Feldwebel	Oberscharführer	Company Sergeant Major	Technical Sergeant
Oberfeldwebel	Hauptscharführer	Sergeant Major	Master Sergeant
Hauptfeldwebel	Stabsscharführer	RSM	First Sergeant
Stabsfeldwebel	Sturmscharführer	Staff Sergeant	Master Sergeant
Leutnant	Untersturmführer	2nd Lieutenant	2nd Lieutenant
Oberleutnant	Obersturmführer	Lieutenant	1st Lieutenant
Hauptmann	Hauptsturmführer	Captain	Captain
Major	Sturmbannführer	Major	Major
Oberstleutnant	Obersturmbannführer	Lieutenant Colonel	Lieutenant Colonel
Oberst	Standartenführer	Colonel	Colonel
—	Oberführer	Brigadier	Brigadier-General
Generalmajor	Brigadeführer	Major General	Brigadier-General
Generalleutnant	Gruppenführer	Lieutenant General	Major General
General der Infantrie (3)	Obergruppenführer	General	Lieutenant-General
Generaloberst	Oberstgruppenführer	General	General
Generalfeldmarschall	Reichführer der SS	Field Marshal	General of Army
		No equivalent	No equivalent

NOTES

(1) Term for 'Riflemen'. From late 1942 all riflemen became Grenadiers. In other arms the equivalent was 'Pioneer' (Engineers), 'Reiter' (Cavalry), 'Jager' (Light Infantry/Mountain Troops), Kanonier (Artillery).

(2) Or 'Obergrenadier,' etc.

(3) Or 'General der Artillerie,' 'General der Kavallerie,' 'General der Panzertruppe,' etc.

DECORATIONS AND SPECIAL BADGES

RIGHT: A much decorated Unteroffizier wearing a Close Combat Clasp in silver on his left breast above the pockets and two Tank Destruction badges on his right sleeve. This special decoration was awarded for the single-handed destruction of a tank by use of normal infantry weapons only; the badge was an aluminium-coloured ribbon with black edging and a miniature tank emblem. On his breast, partly obscured, this soldier is also wearing either the Infantry Assault badge (see below) or the similar Tank Assault badge which is shown at the foot of the page. (IWM).

ABOVE LEFT: The Iron Cross 2nd Class was the most widely awarded of the four classes of Iron Cross. The swastika and date 1939 distinguished it from the first world war Iron Cross. The ribbon of dark red flanked with white and black bars was normally worn in the second button hole of the tunic in service dress, the cross itself not being worn. ABOVE CEN-

TRE: Panzer unit marksmanship shield (awarded to AFV gunners). ABOVE RIGHT: Infantry Assault Badge. Worn on left breast; awarded for three successful attacks on different days. LEFT: Tank Assault Badge. Awarded initially for 3 successful actions but from July 1943 extra grades were issued for 25 (far left), 50, 75, and 100 actions.

Medical personnel
(Sanitätsunterpersonal)

 Saddler candidate
(Truppensattlermeister-Anwärter)

 Paymaster candidate
(Anwärter für die Heeres-Zahlmeisterlaufbahn)

 Motor maintenance sergeant (harness
sergeant if horse outfit)
(Schirrmeister)

 Horseshoeing instructor
(Hufbeschlaglehrmeister)

 Horseshoers (personnel)
(Hufbeschlagpersonal)

 Radio sergeant
(Funkmeister)

 Ordnance sergeant
(Waffenmeister)

 Fortification maintenance sergeant
(Wallmeister)

 Pigeoneer (sergeant)
(Brieftaubenmeister)

 Pyrotechnician
(Feuerwerker)

 Fortification construction sergeant
(Festungspionier-Feldwebel)

 Helmsman (Steuermann). This insignia is worn
on the *left upper* sleeve. (Anchor in silver embroidery)

 Operator smoke troops (Bedienungspersonal Nebel-
abteilung). This insignia is worn on the *left
lower* arm. Worked in white rayon on dark green
background

 Communication personnel (other than Signal Corps)
(Nachrichtenpersonal). This insignia is worn on
the *left upper* sleeve. (Flash in "Waffenfarben")

 Army mountain guide (Heeresbergführer). Thi
insignia is worn on the *left breast*

Gunlayer artillery (Richtkanonier). This insignia
is worn on *left lower* arm

 SPECIALIST BADGES: *Worn by specialist NCOs from Unteroffizier upwards on lower right sleeve except where stated above. See picture on page 7. Embroidered yellow on dark green cloth background (US Official).*

Part 4: Equipment and Weapons

A FULL description of German weapons and infantry equipment is beyond the scope of this present volume. However, this section illustrates the most important infantry weapons and the soldiers' personal equipment.

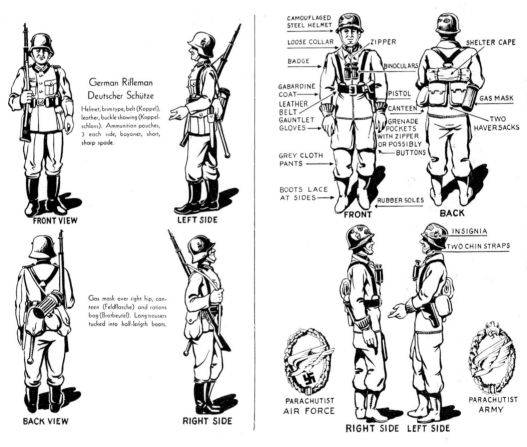

German Rifleman
Deutscher Schütze

Helmet, brim type, belt (Koppel), leather, buckle showing (Koppelschloss). Ammunition pouches, 3 each side, bayonet, short, sharp spade.

FRONT VIEW

LEFT SIDE

Gas mask over right hip, canteen (Feldflasche) and rations bag (Brotbeutel). Long trousers tucked into half-length boots.

BACK VIEW

RIGHT SIDE

CAMOUFLAGED STEEL HELMET
LOOSE COLLAR
BADGE
GABARDINE COAT
LEATHER BELT
GAUNTLET GLOVES
GREY CLOTH PANTS
BOOTS LACE AT SIDES
ZIPPER
BINOCULARS
PISTOL
CANTEEN
GRENADE POCKETS WITH ZIPPER OR POSSIBLY BUTTONS
RUBBER SOLES
FRONT

SHELTER CAPE
GAS MASK
TWO HAVERSACKS
BACK

INSIGNIA
TWO CHIN STRAPS

PARACHUTIST AIR FORCE

RIGHT SIDE LEFT SIDE

PARACHUTIST ARMY

LEFT: Basic personal equipment and accoutrements worn by German infantry man. Hide pack, worn on centre of rear braces in marching order, is omitted. RIGHT: Army or Luftwaffe parachute officer or senior NCO in fighting order. Drawings from US official recognition charts.

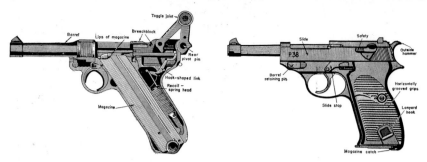

ABOVE LEFT: The well-known Luger (shown in cross-section) was the most common pistol used by the Germans. It was a 9 mm calibre semi-automatic 8 shot weapon. ABOVE RIGHT: Walther P.38 was an 8 shot pistol of 9 mm calibre which partially superseded the Luger in use (US Official).

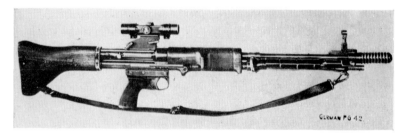

ABOVE: The Fallschirmjager Gewehr 42 (FG 42) was an automatic rifle for paratroops. It was of 7.29 mm calibre and had a rate of fire of 800 rpm (IWM). The standard infantry small arms were the MP 38 and MP 40 sub-machine guns and the Mauser Kar 98k rifle. These are shown in many other pictures in this book.

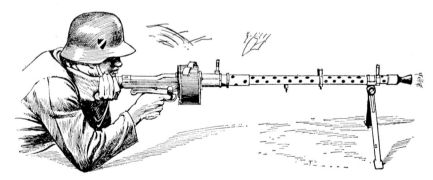

ABOVE: The MG 34 was the standard infantry machine gun. It was an air-cooled weapon of 7.92 mm calibre and with a high cyclic rate of fire. In the 'light machine gun' role it was fired from its folding bipod legs. Shown is a 75 round saddle-type drum magazine. The alternative was a 50 round belt feed (US Official).

RIGHT: In the 'heavy machine gun' role the MG 34 was mounted on a folding tripod mount. It is seen here with belt feed being used by paratroops (IWM).

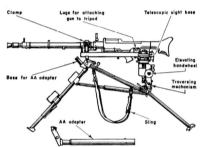

Clamp · Lugs for attaching gun to tripod · Telescopic sight base · Elevating handwheel · Base for AA adapter · Traversing mechanism · AA adapter · Sling

LEFT: A diagram of the MG 34 on the tripod mount. Note carrying sling for folded mount. The same tripod with legs extended and the AA adaptor fitted converted the gun for the anti-aircraft role (US Official).

RIGHT: The MG 42 appeared later in the war as a partial replacement for the MG 34. It was similar to the latter but simplified and refined in design. It had a squarer section barrel jacket compared to the MG 34.

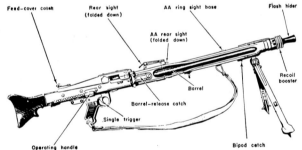

Feed-cover catch · Rear sight (folded down) · AA ring sight base · Flash hider · AA rear sight (folded down) · Barrel · Recoil booster · Barrel-release catch · Single trigger · Operating handle · Bipod catch

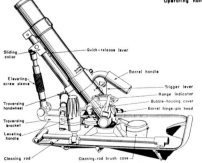

Sliding collar · Quick-release lever · Barrel handle · Elevating-screw sleeve · Trigger lever · Range indicator · Bubble-housing cover · Traversing handwheel · Barrel hinge-pin head · Traversing bracket · Leveling handle · Cleaning rod · Cleaning-rod brush case

LEFT: Standard light mortar was the 5 cm l.gr.W. 36. It was trigger-fired and had a crew of three and maximum range of 568 yards. It broke into two parts (barrel and base-plate) for carrying. Weight was 31 pounds (US Official).

RIGHT: Assault engineers in action, with the most common type of portable flamethrower, the Model 40, carried by the centre man. This equipment was slung in a web harness, weighed 47 pounds and had a 30 yard range (IWM).

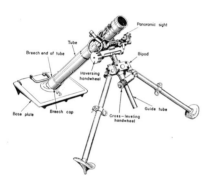

LEFT: Standard heavy infantry mortar was the 8 cm (81 mm) Gr.W. 34 which had a maximum range of 2,078 yards, weighed 125 pounds, and broke into three parts for transportation. BELOW: Organization of a typical infantry regiment (equivalent to a British brigade) (US Official).

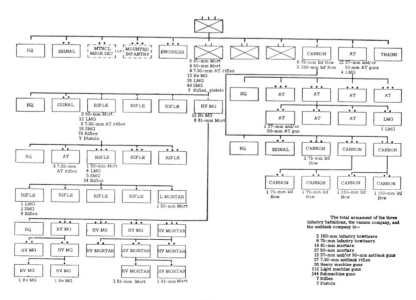

The total armament of the three infantry battalions, the cannon company, and the antitank company is—

2 150-mm infantry howitzers
6 75-mm infantry howitzers
18 81-mm mortars
27 50-mm mortars
12 37-mm and/or 50-mm antitank guns
27 7.92-mm antitank rifles
36 Heavy machine guns
112 Light machine guns
144 Submachine guns
7 Rifles
7 Pistols

48